CONTENTS

Tourist Information Centres

Plymouth's Barbican (Tel: 306330) and Plymouth Discovery Centre at Marsh Mills, adjacent to Sainsburys (Tel: 266030/1)

Summer Opening:
Monday to Saturday 9am - 5pm
Sundays and Bank Holidays 10am - 4 pm

Winter Opening:
Monday to Friday 9am - 5 pm
Saturday 10am - 4 pm
Sunday – closed

Colleges

The University of Plymouth
Drake Circus (Tel: 600600)
Plymouth College of Art and Design
Tavistock Place (Tel: 203434)
Plymouth College of Further Education
Kings Road, Devonport (Tel: 305300)
College of St. Mark & St. John
Derriford (Tel: 777188 or 636700)

Getting About

By Road

The A38 DEVON EXPRESSWAY links Plymouth to the motorway network at Exeter.

TRAVELINE (Tel: 0870.6082608) for details of all bus and coach services in the South West.

PLYMOUTH CITYBUS and FIRST DEVON & CORNWALL provide a comprehensive network of public transport routes. Free citywide route maps are readily available (Tel: 307790).

'DISCOVERER' Services 25 and 25A link Milehouse Park & Ride, the Railway Station, City Centre, historic Barbican and the Hoe. Entry discounts to attractions are available. Rail passengers can buy a through ticket.

Parking

The City Centre has meters and 'pay & display' car parks but, owing to limited parking in the Barbican area, it is a good idea to leave your vehicle in the multi-storey car park at Coxside and walk across the lock gates.

Park & Ride

Facilities are available at Coypool (near Marsh Mills roundabout) and Milehouse (follow signs to Plymouth Argyle). Parking is free at the supervised car parks with good value fares for bus journeys into the city centre. Buses run frequently, every day except Sundays. For obvious reasons, there is no Saturday service from Milehouse when Plymouth Argyle F.C. is playing a home match.

By Rail

PLYMOUTH RAILWAY STATION (Tel:0845.7484950) is on the main London / Penzance railway line, with connections throughout Devon and Cornwall. There is also a picturesque branch line from Plymouth to Gunnislake in Cornwall.

By Air

AIR SOUTH WEST (Tel: 0870.2418202) operates from Plymouth City Airport to Gatwick, Bristol, Manchester, Jersey and Leeds.

AIR WALES (Tel: 0870.7773131) operates from Plymouth City Airport to Dublin, Cork, Cardiff, Newcastle, Liverpool and Aberdeen.

By Sea

BRITTANY FERRIES, Millbay Docks (Tel: 08705.360360)
SUTTON HARBOUR MARINA (Tel: 204186)
QUEEN ANNE'S BATTERY MARINA (Tel: 671142)
MAYFLOWER INTERNATIONAL MARINA (Tel: 556633)
PLYMOUTH YACHT HAVEN (Tel: 404231)
PLYMOUTH BOAT CRUISES (Tel: 822797)
TAMAR CRUISING (Tel: 822105)

Opening Times

*Details and references to displays correct
at time of going to print. Ring to confirm details.*

Plymouth Dome, Hoe Rd (Tel: 603300)
Open April to Oct. 10 - 5pm.
Winter 10 - 4pm. (closed Sun & Mon).
Last entry 1 hour before closing.

Smeaton's Tower, The Hoe
Discounted combined entry tickets with Dome (above).
Open April to end Sept. 10 - 4pm.
Winter 10 - 3pm. (closed Sun & Mon).

National Marine Aquarium, Barbican(Tel: 220084)
Open every day except Christmas.
Summer 10 - 6pm. Winter 10 - 5pm.

City Museum & Art Gallery, Tavistock Rd (Tel: 304774)
Open all year.
Tues to Fri 10 - 5.30pm. Sat. & Bank Holidays. 10 - 5pm.

Merchant's House, 33, St. Andrew's St (Tel: as above)
Open Easter to end Sept. 10 - 5pm. (closed Sun & Mon).

Elizabethan House, 32, New St, Barbican (Tel: 253871)
Open Easter to end Sept. 10 - 5pm. (closed Sun & Mon) .

Plymouth Mayflower, 3/5, The Barbican (Tel: 306330)
Open May to Oct. 10 - 4pm.
Nov. to Apr. 10 - 4pm. Closed Sun.

Prysten House, behind St. Andrew's Church (Tel: 661414)
Openings by arrangement with Church Office.
Tanners Restaurant on ground floor and in courtyard.

The Royal Citadel, The Hoe
Admission by arrangement - for details,
contact the Tourist Information Centre.

Black Friars Distillery, 60, Southside St (Tel: 665292)
Plymouth Gin Company open daily for tours & tastings.

The Guildhall, Royal Parade (Tel: 307963)
Visits by arrangement, when not in Civic use.

Crownhill Fort, Tavistock Rd (Tel: 793754)
Open April to Sept. for weekend events.
Phone for details.

Mount Edgcumbe House, Cremyll (Tel: 822236)
Open April to end Sept. 11 - 4.30pm. Closed Fri & Sat.
Gardens and Parkland open all year.

Cotehele House, near Calstock (Tel: 01579.351346)
Open Easter to Oct. 11 - 5pm. Closed Fri.
Garden open all year from 10.30am to dusk.
Mill opening times vary.

Antony House, Torpoint (Tel: 812191)
Open Easter to Oct. Tues to Thurs 1.30 - 5.30pm.
Also Sundays and Bank Holidays in June, July & Aug.

Saltram House, Plympton (Tel: 333500)
Open Easter to Oct. Closed Fri.
House 12 - 4.30pm.
Garden & tearoom open from 11am.

Buckland Abbey, near Yelverton (Tel: 01822.853607)
Open Easter to Oct. 10.30 - 5.30pm. Closed Thurs.
Winter 2 - 5pm. on Sat & Sun only.
Pre-arranged parties by arrangement.

Morwellham Quay, nr Tavistock (Tel: 01822.832766)
Open every day except Christmas & New Year.
Summer 10 - 5.30pm.
Winter 10 - 4.30pm.

Dartmoor National Park,
Princetown (Tel: 01822.890414)

The Theatre Royal,
Royal Parade. Box Office (Tel: 267222)

Plymouth Pavilions,
Millbay Rd (Tel: 229922)

The Athenaeum Theatre,
Derry's Cross (Tel: 266104)

The Barbican Theatre,
Castle St (Tel: 267131)

Derriford Hospital
(Tel: 777111); A&E Dept (Tel: 792511)

HISTORY OF THE CITY

The City of Plymouth, which lies between the Rivers Plym and Tamar, commands the entrance to the English Channel and has one of the finest natural harbours in the world.

Occupation of this area began at least 20,000 years ago when Stone Age people lived on the northern shore of the Plym estuary. More recently, about 3,000 years ago, the small port of Mount Batten sprang up on the headland opposite and, from there, a thriving community of metal workers and fishermen ran a bustling sea trade with southern Britain and western France. That centre flourished until the end of Roman times but the story of Plymouth itself really began with the Saxons. They set up many manors in the district and one of these, near the mouth of the River Plym, developed into a small fishing village known then by the ancient name of Sudtone (South Farm)

Some time after the Norman Invasion of 1066, control of the town passed into the hands of the wealthy and powerful priors of nearby Plympton, a small but busy port that exported Dartmoor tin. The unfortunate silting up of the River Plym meant that Plympton lost its trade to Sutton (a derivation of the ancient name of Sudtone) and became a backwater that was eventually swallowed up, whilst Sutton grew from an unimportant fishing village into a centre for over-seas trade. The limestone hill we now call the Hoe sheltered it from the prevailing west wind as well as hiding it from marauding pirates.

By the 14th century, Sutton had become known as Plymouth but the old name is still preserved today in one of Plymouth's parliamentary constituencies and also in the name of Sutton Harbour.

After the French raids of the 14th and 15th centuries, Plymouth petitioned Parliament for incorporation, which would have enabled the buying of land needed to build a protective town wall. Permission was refused and so the townsfolk had to fortify their town as best they could. However, a fresh petition in 1439 was successful and Plymouth became the first town in the land to receive a charter by Act of Parliament. This bestowed certain rights upon the citizens, thereby reducing the power of the priors of Plympton and allowing Plymouth to prosper during the following century. In this she was greatly assisted by Drake's influence.

Her value as a naval base had been recognised by Edward I as long ago as the 13th century and the great tradition of seamanship and shipbuilding that developed here meant that, by the 18th century, she was to become known throughout the world.

The present population is approximately 250,000 but many more thousands live in the 43 other Plymouths scattered around the globe. More than 30 of these are in the U.S.A.

The three towns of Plymouth, Devonport and Stonehouse were amalgamated in 1914 and Plymouth was granted city status in 1928. The coat of arms, authorised in 1931, bears the motto 'Turris fortissima est nomen Jehova' which translates as 'The name of the Lord is the strongest tower'. The one pictured here appears on the Plymouth side of the Tamar Road Bridge. On the Cornish side there is a crest depicting a fisherman, a miner and a chough.

The City Coat of Arms

Over the years many famous names have been associated with the City: - Sir Francis Drake, Sir Richard Grenville, William Hawkins, Sir John Hawkins, Sir Humphrey Gilbert, Sir Walter Raleigh, Sir Martin Frobisher, Sir Joshua Reynolds, William Cookworthy, Tobias Furneaux, Captain Cook, Charles Darwin, Scott of the Antarctic, Lady Nancy Astor and Sir Francis Chichester, to name but a few, and each has left a footprint on the history of Plymouth.

St. Andrew's Church

St. Andrew's Church

This, the largest parish church in the County of Devon, is the mother church of Plymouth. The name is particularly appropriate since St. Andrew is the patron saint of fishermen and Plymouth actually began its life as a small fishing village. Because he was crucified on an X-shaped cross, this form is known as a St. Andrew's cross, or saltire, and that appears on the City's coat of arms.

There are records of a church on this site in Saxon times but the oldest part of the present building is the South Chapel, built about 1385. The main structure of the walls is 15th century. Under the chancel, a crypt belonging to an earlier church was discovered which contained a Purbeck Stone figure approximately 750 years old. The tower was built in 1461 using materials provided by a wealthy and pious resident, Thomas Yogge, who later built the Prysten House (see page 6). The church contains interesting memorials and the heart of Sir Martin Frobisher, first British navigator to find the North West passage through the Arctic seas.

The parish church of St. Andrew was at the heart of the ancient settlement of Sutton Prior and, as we pause here for a moment, we realise that this church would have heard the grateful prayers of the successful sea captains after their victory over the Spanish Armada, the hopeful prayers of the Pilgrim Fathers before they left for America, and the pleas of the townsfolk who would have met here for mutual succour in the dark years of the siege of Plymouth during the Civil War.

St. Andrew's possesses a complete set of baptismal, marriage and burial registers dating from 1581. Fortunately, these survived the awful Blitz of March 1941 when much of the ancient town centre was completely obliterated. The church itself was gutted by fire and so badly damaged that only its medieval shell remained. Within hours of the destruction, a board bearing the word RESURGAM was fixed over the north door. It means 'I shall rise again' and this single word became an inspiration to Plymothians as they set about rebuilding their city as well as their church.

The Garden Church (Beauty from the Ashes)

Beds of flowers were planted inside its walls and, as a result, it became known as The Garden Church. Here the tradition of worship was kept alive until restoration work began in 1949.

Reconsecration of the church took place on St. Andrew's Day, November 30th, in 1957.

The Prysten House

This fine example of 15th century architecture stands in Finewell Street, behind St. Andrew's Church, and is the oldest house in central Plymouth. Although it is popularly linked with the visiting priests who came from Plympton Priory to minister at St. Andrew's, the true priests' house actually stood further down Finewell Street.

Built between 1487 and 1498, this house was known, until the 19th century, as Yogges House. Thomas Yogge was a wealthy merchant who imported wines from France and stored them in Plymouth prior to distribution around the country. When the burghers of the town set up a cartel to squeeze out 'foreign' merchants, Yogge, who was Cornish, moved to London but continued to use Plymouth as his base. The new contacts he made in the Capital greatly assisted the distribution of his wines and he became even more successful. It is generally accepted that he commissioned the building of this house, the very finest in the town and situated right next to St. Andrew's Church, as a snub to the town's burghers.

The house, of limestone with granite door and window frames, is built around three sides of an unique galleried courtyard and contains certain architectural features of the south-east of England where Yogge then lived. Whether or not Thomas Yogge ever returned to live in this house we can't be sure but we do know that he used it to lodge his business contacts - wine merchants from

other parts of the country as well as those over from France.

At various times the building has been used as a dwelling house, a wine store (about 1800), a warehouse (about 1900) and, most recently, as a bacon factory.

The present transformation came after the First World War. There were firm expectations that Plymouth would become a Cathedral City and this presented a problem because there was no Church Hall or other building that could be used as cathedral offices. The Prysten House was ideally situated for this purpose so the congregation of St. Andrew's bought and restored it. Then, using the same architectural style, Abbey Hall was constructed onto the rear. The two blend so well together that it is hard to believe that this addition was built as recently as 1923.

Plymouth did not become a Cathedral City but we can be grateful to that expectation because it preserved the Prysten House for us. It is now open to the public and worth visiting to see the limestone well (Finewell), the circular stone staircases and the 28ft. Plymouth Tapestry. This beautiful piece of work, created by volunteer embroiderers using Gobelin stitchwork, was started in 1977 and took 4½ years to complete, using an estimated 2,250,000 stitches.

The Plymouth Tapestry

The subject was taken from the minutes of the Old White Book of Plymouth Corporation for July 21st 1561, when the council agreed to appoint its first schoolmaster, one Thomas Brooke. The names of those who contributed to the building of the school and the amounts they paid are recorded, along with the names of the twelve Aldermen and the twenty-four Councillors. The golden key after some of the names indicates that these were the holders of the four keys to the town's castle. Whenever an alarm was sounded, it was their responsibility to unlock the armoury and distribute the weapons.

Today the ancient limestone Finewell is centrepiece to an excellent restaurant named Tanners.

The Door of Unity is the main doorway of the Prysten House. Beside it stands a tombstone mounted on a granite panel, a memorial restored by the American Society of the Daughters of 1812 who are descendants of the American prisoners of war. It commemorates the chivalrous act of 1813 when, after a battle in Plymouth Sound between H.M.S. Pelican and U.S.N. Brig Argus, two American officers were brought ashore and buried with respect in St. Andrew's. It bears the words 'Here sleep the brave'. Each year a service is held here on the last Friday in November.

At Saltash Passage, on the banks of the River Tamar, stands a more recent U.S. memorial, marking the departure of soldiers for the 'D-Day' landings in Northern France in June 1944.

THE DOOR OF UNITY

The Merchant's House

This fine Tudor residence is early 16th century. Between its massive limestone side walls are moulded oak-framed windows that run almost the full width of the building. The first and second floors jut out, supported on granite corbels. The entrance, through a recessed granite archway, looks rather small in comparison. The reason the house is so long and narrow is that, at the time it was being built, plots were paid for by the length of their frontage.

It was significantly altered and embellished at the start of the 17th century by William Parker, an Elizabethan privateer who, like Drake, had raided the Spaniards and brought back great wealth to the City. Parker later became Mayor of Plymouth and lived in this house from 1608 so it is probable that loot taken from the Spanish treasure fleet in the Caribbean paid for its renovation. Records show that at least two other mayors also lived in this house in the 17th century.

As one would expect of a house of this age, it had passed through many hands. At one time it was a pram factory and, most recently, a taxi office. Sadly, time had taken its toll and it was in a very sorry state of repair when James Barber, then director of the City Museum, stepped in. The building had been condemned and was actually on the point of being demolished. His intervention was in the nick of time and it is only through his enthusiasm and persistence that the house still stands today. He literally saved this house for the City and it rightly stands as a memorial to him.

With as many as possible of the original features retained and made good, the building was finally opened to the public in 1978. Today it is the largest and finest example of this period left in the city and serves as a museum of Plymouth history. Its exhibits include a fabulously furnished dolls house from a wealthy Victorian home, a penny-farthing bicycle, a Victorian pharmacy which is utterly charming and where, if you are lucky, you can see pill rolling being demonstrated, and an extremely rare ducking stool made of metal. This once stood on the Barbican quayside, near the Mayflower Steps, and used to be lowered into the sea on a jib. Last but not least there is a Victorian schoolroom to which children are brought from schools as far afield as Bristol and Penzance to be given a taste of the Victorian method of education. Girls wearing white cotton pinafores and boys in jackets of the period sit in old wooden desks, writing with steel-nibbed pens and chanting multiplication tables, whilst the 'Victorian headmaster' blows his whistle and occasionally thrashes his long cane on a desk...just for effect.

Around the corner, in Notte Street, a restaurant now stands on the site of William Cookworthy's house. He was an apothecary and the first Englishman to discover the ancient Chinese secret of porcelain manufacture.

Across the road, at the top of Hoegate Street, a plaque marks the site of Hoe Gate, one of the old town gateways which was the last to be removed, having stood there from 1593 to 1862.

Penny-farthing Bicycle

Ducking Stool

The Barbican

Today the name Barbican refers to the whole of the waterside area around Sutton Harbour. Originally, barbican meant an outer fortification and would have referred to an outer defence of the ancient castle that once dominated the entrance to the harbour.

Here, midst the narrow cobbled alleyways and stepped lanes, there is much to attract the visitor - antique shops and art galleries, pubs and eating houses, small shops tucked inside old warehouses, a bake house with its original 17th century oven and even a little theatre housed in a building that was once a seaman's Bethel Mission. Built in 1883, it turned theatrical in the 1950s and today offers a small and intimate forum for youth and community theatre.

Although old names such as Damnation Alley, Tin Street, Pike Street and Dung Lane have all disappeared now, here and there little treasures of buildings from the past still catch the eye and delight the beholder. Note the delightful 17th century house in Southside Street, made of timber frame with overhang, with its moulded doorframe providing passage to a rear courtyard.

Black Friars Distillery

The Distillery is one of the oldest buildings in Plymouth, with parts of the original structure dating back to about 1430. Dominican friars, who wore black cloaks, had no friary in Plymouth but the Franciscans, who wore grey cloaks and were consequently known as Grey Friars, did have a site nearby - so maybe it should be called Grey Friars Distillery? Carmelites, White Friars, had a friary near Charles Church and are remembered today in the name of Friary Court near St. Jude's Church.

The ornate stone carving of the original low doorway is a beautiful example of the English Perpendicular architectural style but today's entrance is via the cobblestoned street that once stood beside it. The old flagstones, ramps and drainage grooves are still

Southside Street

there, as are the mullioned windows and granite doorways which nowadays open onto a covered courtyard with a stairway leading to the Refectory Room, a splendid medieval hall with a fine hull-shaped timber roof. The timbers of this arch-braced roof date back to 1430, so take a look.

The building was probably one of Plymouth's several guildhalls and was, at one time, used as the town's Marshalsea or Debtor's Prison. It was also the first Non-Conformist meeting place, a billet for Huguenot refugees and, it is believed, the last meeting place of the Pilgrim Fathers before they set sail on the Mayflower in 1620.

Today Black Friars Distillery is the home of the famous Plymouth Gin, the only one still produced at its original distillery. Since it began in 1793, production methods have changed little. Here, England's oldest working distillery creates a delightfully smooth gin of great aroma and complexity, still handcrafted in ancient copper pots and still to the original recipe. A glass partition at the back of the cobblestoned entrance gives a fascinating glimpse of the two enormous 19th century stills and, if this whets the appetite, guided tours and tastings are available all year round. It is well worth a visit, not only to enjoy a cocktail in the architectural splendour of the Refectory Room but also to see and experience how this unique gin is made.

Experts claim that Plymouth Gin's exceptionally fresh taste is thanks to the crystal clear Dartmoor water that is used in its production. It is interesting to note that the soft water from springs around the Barbican and Union Street made the town a popular place for the production of beer, gin and soft drinks. There have been over 150 such manufacturers operating in Plymouth in the past 100 years or so.

Black Friars Distillery

Sutton Harbour

Southside Street is the main thoroughfare of the Barbican and, behind it, lies Sutton Harbour. In 1337, Edward III gave Sutton Pool to the Duchy of Cornwall which, in 1891, sold it to the Sutton Harbour Company for £38,000. At one time it was just a ragged line of warehouses with their feet in the water but the construction of Vauxhall Quay in 1602 transformed the area.

From the 13th century onwards, Plymouth grew from an unimportant fishing village into a centre for overseas trade. The inlet reached up to the buildings at the far end but, by 1520, it had been completely filled in. After 1775 this in-fill was used as a parade ground by the Marines who used to billet in houses around the Barbican area before the present barracks at Stonehouse was built, which explains its name 'The Parade'.

The three finely decorated fireplaces embedded in the wall of Basket Ope are early 17th century but Hawkins' great house which, in 1608, stood on the opposite side of Vauxhall Street, is sadly no longer there. This area was once rich in Tudor and Jacobean houses.

Nearby you see the mullioned windows and granite doorways of the old Custom House (built 1586) and opposite, the present Custom House (built 1820). The Three Crowns was built in the early 1600s, probably as a dwelling house and, although it has had a Georgian face-lift, it still shows signs of its early origins. Its name commemorates the union of the three crowns of England, Scotland and Ireland under James I (James VI of Scotland).

By the mid 19th century, congestion caused by the emigration ships and the booming fishing industry (7,352 tons of fish were landed in 1892) made it necessary to widen the quay near the Mayflower Steps. The line of the old Barbican sea wall is shown by the change in the cobbles. Most of the granite edged quays around the harbour were re-built or extended in the 19th century. In 1896, a fish market was built on this reclaimed land. Its designer, Sir John Inglis, was engineer for Great Western Railway which explains why the building, with its cast-iron columns and wood-trimmed roof, so resembles a railway station. Note the redbrick Railway Office opposite and the remains of Brunel's G.W.R. broad gauge railway lines which are still visible along Sutton Wharf and North Quay.

In 1995 the Fish Market moved across to the other side of Sutton Harbour and the old fish quay became home to the Barbican Glassworks, operated by Dartington Crystal.

Left of the new Fish Market stand quays that were used in the late 18th century for the shipment of pottery and porcelain. This would have certainly included the famous Plymouth Porcelain produced between 1768 and 1774 by Cookworthy; the first time 'true' hard-paste porcelain had been produced in Britain. Some 50 to 60 people were employed in its production. The building with the veranda is the China House, dating from about 1650, sole survivor of three storehouses which once stood there and one of the very few left in the country. Although originally built as a warehouse, it has had many and varied uses - naval storehouse, gun wharf, hospital, prison, timber store, shipbuilding yard and vehicle repair workshop. Today it is an attractive waterside pub/restaurant, bursting with atmosphere.

From late medieval times Sutton Pool was a busy thriving harbour but, by the mid 20th century, it had fallen into disuse. Today the old warehouses have taken on a new lease of life as shops, pubs and restaurants, and are once again a vital part of Barbican life.

having large mullioned windows that span the entire width of the building so as to catch as much light as possible. Glass panes were set in lead to allow for easy replacement. The second and third storeys project out, resting on carved oak corbels, and the side walls are of limestone into which are set the great chimney pieces so necessary to provide adequate heating. These still boast their original cobbled hearths paved with pebbles from the local shore, each room in a different pattern. The inglenook fireplace in the rear kitchen would have housed a dog-spit prior to the invention of mechanical jacks. A passageway leading from the front door through to the enclosed courtyard and terraced garden has a panelled oak partition dividing it from the living quarters, indicating that it once provided access for the properties at the rear.

Beneath the house is a small cellar that can be reached from a narrow staircase in the corridor or by wooden doors directly from the street (inaccessible to the public). The upper floors are reached via a spiral staircase, a form typical of the Tudor houses in old Plymouth. The central newel post is a disused ship's mast and the heavy rope guide-rail that snakes around it is also a traditional feature. Throughout the years, as these stairs became worn, it was the practice to repair them by placing new treads on top of the old. During the 1881 census, 57 souls were registered as living in this house and those behind it, so it is not surprising to discover that, during the restoration work of the 1920s, four layers of treads were found on these stairs.

The Elizabethan House contains some lovely pieces of furniture, mainly 17th century in origin: - an inlaid writing desk, strangely tall by modern standards because writing was originally done from a standing position; a heavy iron chest, reinforced with metal bands, which would have been used to store valuables such as money, title deeds and perhaps jewellery; a large oak settle with back and sides to protect from draughts; a lockable spice cabinet; and a carved oak bible box. The ventilated livery cupboard (wall pantry) on the first floor would have been used to store candles as well as food. The rush lights of those days lasted only about 30 minutes so the precious beeswax and tallow candles would almost certainly have been locked away. Perishable foodstuffs would have been pickled, preserved in barrels of salt, or bottled and sealed with resin.

Amongst the period furniture in the bedrooms are carved oak chests, a canopied 16th century four-poster bed, a cradle that rocks quite violently with no apparent human assistance and a box-bed made in Brittany in 1649 with a sliding door (for privacy as well as warmth) and adjustable rope supports - hence the expression 'sleep tight'.

Personal hygiene was not as we know it today. Frequent washing and baths were a rarity, teeth were cleaned by rubbing with a cloth, sometimes using mint to freshen the breath, and quick lime or urine was used to bleach clothes when washing - which took place approximately four times a year, whether they needed it or not.

In the 1800s, most of the rear gardens of New Street contained squalid, overcrowded dwellings but these were demolished by the 1930s. Today, behind numbers 34 - 40, there is an Elizabethan Garden - a quiet haven on varying levels with knot and rose gardens, a pool and the 1630 entrance to the Hospital of the Poor's Portion.

The Elizabethan House

This beautiful house, along with 19th century warehouses and bonded stores, stands in New Street - one of the oldest streets in the City! Next-door stands Palace Vaults, built in 1809 to store prizes taken by the Navy during the Napoleonic wars. New Street was actually new in the late 1500s, a time when Plymouth was a prosperous, bustling port teeming with sailors, merchants and foreign privateers. This was the very heart of the town's commercial and sea-going life. Between 1575 and 1660 the population had doubled and so there was need for new housing. New Street was a part of that development, though it was known then as Grey Friar Street because of the friary that stood at the far end. These were not houses built for the wealthy but homes for ordinary merchants and sea captains. The wealthy lived in larger properties on the other side of town. Southside Street was also part of that Elizabethan expansion, as was Looe Street, the top of which is the site of Drake's old house. It is also home to the Minerva Inn, the oldest pub in the City.

By 1929 the Elizabethan house was a condemned, boarded-up slum but it was rescued from demolition and, in 1930, opened to the public as a museum. It gives visitors a vivid impression of Plymouth as it was in Drake's day and contains some carved oak features recovered from less fortunate houses in the surrounding Barbican area. The nearness of the house opposite shows why fire and plague spread so easily. Although other Elizabethan properties have survived in this narrow, granite-cobbled street (N.B. the continuous row between 34 and 40 with carved wooden door frames) number 32 is rare in that it has survived almost complete since its construction in 1584.

The front is of oak timber-frame construction, the first two floors

The Pilgrim Fathers

Overlooking Sutton Harbour stands Island House, an imposing building with gables and stuccoed timber frame that dates from the late 16th century. It is reputed to have lodged some of the Pilgrim Fathers before they set sail for America in 1620.

The sailing was not a West Country project. Indeed, it was only storm damage that brought them into Plymouth at all. The Pilgrim movement had begun in Nottinghamshire some 40 years earlier. They wanted a simpler, more godly way of living. They had a strict moral code and discipline was important - church attendance was imposed by law. By 1606 a separatist church had been formed and, as a result, heavy fines were imposed with some Pilgrims being imprisoned. To avoid persecution, they left England for Holland where they would have the freedom to worship as they chose and live according to their strict Puritan rules. However, worries about losing their mother tongue and becoming engulfed by the Dutch way of life made them decide to go to America.

Permission was obtained from James I to establish a settlement in the New World so, after 12 years in Holland, they set sail from Delft Haven in the 60-ton Speedwell, to be joined at Southampton by the 180-ton Mayflower. The Speedwell soon proved to be unseaworthy and had to be abandoned. Although some disheartened passengers gave up, the rest joined the Mayflower when it left from Plymouth.

The Mayflower had a keel length of less than 60ft (18.5 metres) with only 4ft 9ins headroom (1.45 metres). There were 150 people on board (102 passengers + 48 crew) and, since there were no portholes, passengers were forced to spend the 67 days' journey in semi-darkness with very little fresh air. The limited space was also shared by chickens, goats, pigs and dogs that they had taken with them. As if that weren't enough, the tiny little Mayflower also carried essentials such as furniture and cooking pots. During this long and extremely uncomfortable journey the sleeping quarters were constantly wet and they survived on salt beef, dried fish, biscuits, cheese and beer. One poor woman even gave birth under those dreadful conditions.

The Pilgrims had intended to settle in Virginia but stormy weather forced them to land on December 20th (now called Fore-Fathers' Day) at Plymouth, Massachusetts. This was pure coincidence and not named by them as is commonly believed. The following day was a Sunday and a special thanksgiving service was held. They had crossed the mighty Atlantic in a tiny ship no bigger than 2 buses.

During the following year, almost half died of some unknown disease. The remainder survived by working on a communal basis, greatly aided by the local Indians who helped them obtain wild game and fish and well as showing them how to grow maize and beans. They also began rearing turkeys and today this forms the basis of the Thanksgiving dinner that Americans eat each year at the end of November to commemorate that very first harvest in the New World.

Island House

It had been a severe winter, full of hardship, but no one chose to return with the Mayflower when she sailed back to England. Later, the Pilgrims expressed their gratitude to the Plymothians who had displayed such kindness to them in the days before their departure.

The board fixed to the outside of Island House contains the names of some of the courageous Pilgrims who made that epic voyage across the Atlantic and helped to found a nation.

Plymouth Mayflower

The Tourist Information Office can be found on the ground floor of this modern building. It also houses an interpretation centre that tells the story of the Pilgrim Fathers and the Mayflower, as well as the creation of Sutton Harbour itself. Interactive graphics explore this working harbour through the ages with tales of merchant families, the fishing industry, the military harbour and emigration to the New World. Here visitors can sample the life of Plymouth's bustling Barbican maritime village, both past and present.

Plymouth Mayflower

East and West Piers

These piers, built between 1791 and 1799, stand at the entrance to Sutton Harbour, the centre of Plymouth's seafaring life until well into the 19th century. West Pier probably incorporated some of the 17th century Cawsey, the pier from which the Pilgrim Fathers actually embarked in 1620. The arch, pictured here, commemorates that departure. The nearby pub is named after Admiral John McBride, M.P. for Plymouth, who organised the government grant that paid for the construction of the piers. Memorials to fishermen adorn the wall below the old Boatman's Shelter, once a place where they waited out bad weather conditions and now, appropriately, home to the R.N.L.I. shop.

Mayflower Steps

From April to October boat-trips that leave from the Mayflower Steps and Phoenix Wharf offer a chance to see the city from a different perspective. There are short excursions to see the warships in the Naval Dockyard, a water-taxi over to Mount Batten, cruises up the River Tamar and, during peak season, excursions to Cawsand, Looe and up the Yealm River.

Some of the plaques dotted around West Pier commemorate: -

Sir Humphrey Gilbert's 1583 departure for Newfoundland, England's first colonial possession.

Richard Grenville's departure and subsequent colonisation of the Roanoke Colonies in 1584. Jamestown is the oldest English settlement on the North American mainland. This land, named Virginia in honour of Elizabeth I, is now known as North Carolina.

The 1609 voyage of the ill-fated Sea Venture, flagship of a small fleet of English ships bound for Virginia which was devastated by a hurricane. The capsizing of the Sea Venture off Bermuda led to its subsequent colonisation by Sir George Somers and the survivors' story inspired Shakespeare's tale 'The Tempest'.

The departure, in 1787, of transportation ships that carried men and women convicts bound for Australia. They landed at Port Jackson, later to become Sydney, where they established the first British colony.

The Laying of the new iron pipes in 1826 which improved Drake's original fresh water supply of 1591.

THE TOLPUDDLE MARTYRS.

THIS PLAQUE. PLACED HERE BY MEMBERS OF THE VARIOUS TRADES UNIONS AFFILIATED TO THE PLYMOUTH AND DISTRICT TRADES COUNCIL COMMEMORATES THE LANDING NEAR THIS SPOT ON 18TH MARCH 1838
OF
JAMES LOVELESS, JAMES BRINE, THOMAS AND JOHN STANFIELD
(4 OF THE 6 DORSET FARM WORKERS AFTER EXILE IN AUSTRALIA)
Freedom and Justice was their Cause
5TH MAY 956

The 1838 homecoming of the Tolpuddle Martyrs after their transportation overseas for daring to form a trade union.

The departure in May 1839 of the Tory, pioneer ship in the colonisation of New Zealand. The following year, six more carrying 897 emigrants left from Plymouth to found New Plymouth on North Island. During the 19th century thousands left Cornwall to colonise New Zealand and their wealth of mining and farming skills proved to be a great contribution.

The landing in Plymouth Sound of the American seaplane NC4 on completion of the first transatlantic flight in 1919. The seven-day journey had been made in a flying boat with a wingspan of 126ft (39 metres) and weighing only 14 tons fully laden.

A memorial to the 31,442 Merchant Seamen who died in World War II.

A stone crown marking the embarkation of Elizabeth II, in July 1962, on her visit to Plymouth to open the then new Civic Centre.

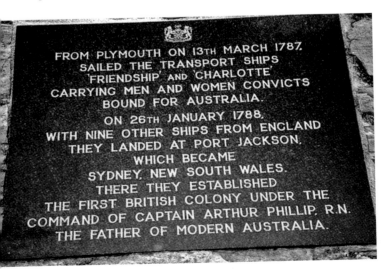

FROM PLYMOUTH ON 13TH MARCH 1787 SAILED THE TRANSPORT SHIPS 'FRIENDSHIP' AND 'CHARLOTTE' CARRYING MEN AND WOMEN CONVICTS BOUND FOR AUSTRALIA.

ON 26TH JANUARY 1788, WITH NINE OTHER SHIPS FROM ENGLAND THEY LANDED AT PORT JACKSON, WHICH BECAME SYDNEY, NEW SOUTH WALES. THERE THEY ESTABLISHED THE FIRST BRITISH COLONY UNDER THE COMMAND OF CAPTAIN ARTHUR PHILLIP. R.N. THE FATHER OF MODERN AUSTRALIA.

Admiral MacBride Pub

In 1768 Captain James Cook, the greatest navigator of the 1700s, departed from Plymouth. In fact, all three of his epic voyages of discovery started from here. In May 1770 he landed in Botany Bay and set about charting the coasts of New Zealand and Western Australia, which he claimed for Britain. This was followed, in 1772, by a second successful voyage but the third, in 1776, ended in tragedy - at the age of 51 he was killed by Hawaiian warriors. Cook was meticulous and did more than any other to map the surface of the globe.

It was from Devonport, on the western side of the City, that The Beagle and its famous passenger Charles Darwin departed in 1831 on their epic 5-year voyage. These years working as a naturalist proved most productive. He was constantly observing, collecting and thinking about the geological and biological phenomena that confronted him. During the years after the voyage he read widely and thought deeply, experimenting and assembling evidence and, as a result, 'The Origin of Species' was eventually published in 1859. It caused uproar in Victorian Society. Copies of the book were burned and the author was denounced from the pulpit. He had begun a revolution that split the scientific community. It may be hard for us to believe now but, before that, most biologists thought of species as fixed groups ordained by God. Darwin put forward the principle of natural selection as a plausible mechanism to explain how species can change - how nature guarantees the survival of the fittest.

Plymouth has had an historic and exciting past and its present is still alive with adventure. It is the starting point of the OSTAR (original single-handed trans Atlantic race) to Newport, Rhode Island and of the two-handed round Britain and Ireland Race, both organised by the Royal Western Yacht club of England, and also the finish of the biennial Fastnet Race. The tradition of seamanship lives on.

The National Marine Aquarium

A sculpture representing various sea creatures beckons you across the lock gates to the National Marine Aquarium, the largest aquarium in the U.K. There you are taken on a journey around the world including 3,500 fish from over 200 different species in over 50 live exhibits.

The 'Shore and Shallow Sea' display overlooks Plymouth Sound, which really puts it into context with its natural surroundings, whilst the delightful seahorse exhibit shows more species than anywhere else in the U.K. with examples from around the planet. The cinema-screen sized Atlantic 'Deep Reef' can be viewed on two levels whilst the Mediterranean Tank, the deepest in Europe (10½metres) has sharks that swim over-head. From here you can see the beautiful coloured 'Coral Seas' where hundreds of jewel-bright tropical fish live alongside two black tipped reef sharks and Snorkel, the loggerhead turtle. There is also a viewing bubble where you can get an even closer encounter.

Guides are on hand throughout to answer questions and help you get the most from your visit, and there is a daily programme of talks and presentations. The Aquarium is available for group visits, evening functions, birthday parties etc. but, as well as being great entertainment, it is a centre of excellence for research and conservation work.

The Cattewater

Beyond the lock gates of Sutton Harbour lies a stretch of water known as the Cattewater. This, the lower estuary of the River Plym, is commonly believed to have been so called because Catherine of Aragon landed here in 1501. She was just 15 years old and spent 2 weeks in Plymouth recovering from the voyage before leaving to become the first wife of Henry VIII. His great-grandfather, the Black Prince, had helped Spain throw out the Moors and so England and Spain were good friends…but this was soon to change. However, it had been called the Catte as long ago as the 13th century when it may have taken its name from a local physical feature, probably a rock that resembled a cat.

It was the Cattewater that provided sheltered anchorage for ships prior to the construction of The Breakwater out in Plymouth Sound and it was here that the English Navy lay in wait, in 1588, as the Spanish Armada advanced up The Channel.

Fishing Boats alongside West Pier

The Castle Quadrate Wall

The Castle Quadrate

Plymouth Castle once stood like a sentry at the entrance to Sutton Harbour. The castle quadrant (known in Plymouth as Castle Quadrate) was a rectangular building with a round tower at each corner. Today, these towers appear on the City's coat of arms. Prior to its construction, successive English monarchs had used Plymouth as their naval base. As long ago as the 1200s, Edward I based 325 ships here in order to attack France, so there was an obvious need to protect the town.

During the Hundred Years War, the French attacked the Channel ports. In 1337, a number of ships were burned in Sutton Harbour, part of the town destroyed and 89 men killed. As a result, town defences were strengthened. In 1346, Plymouth aided Edward III in his siege and capture of Calais and in 1355, his son, the Black Prince (first Prince of Wales), used it as his base to defeat the French. Their King John was brought here as prisoner and held ransom for a large area of France. These events provoked retaliation and, about 1380, the castle was built. In 1399, 1400 and 1403 the Breton Raids took place, the worst being the 1403 raid when 30 ships and 1,200 solders landed within a mile of the town and attacked from the rear. This last major battle, said to have resulted in the burning of 600 houses with great loss of life on both sides, is remembered in the use of Bretonside for an ancient street name and the present day coach-station. The Castle was eventually demolished when the Royal Citadel was built in the 1660s.

Shoreline Defences

From the sea, traces of outer defences can still be seen along the water's edge. These probably date from before 1540. Among them is an artillery tower at the point known as Fisher's Nose. During World War II it was used as an A.R.P. shelter but it had been built by Henry VIII to defend against a very different enemy. After 18 years of marriage to Catherine of Aragon, he divorced her for failing to produce an heir and declared himself supreme head of The Church. The ensuing anti-clerical revolution, dissolution of monasteries and redistribution of their wealth made him popular with the people, but fearful of reprisals from the Catholic countries of Europe, so he built a chain of solid, functional forts and batteries to defend landing places from possible invasion. Other such defences can be found at Devil's Point and Mount Edgcumbe. The artillery tower at Firestone Bay, now a restaurant, was built in the late 1400s and therefore pre-dates Henry's fortifications.

The Hoe

The Hoe is made of limestone, part of an ancient coral reef that stretched from Torbay. It is aptly named - Hoe is a Saxon word meaning high place. Today it is a pleasure to stroll along its grassy slopes but years ago it was covered with rough grass on which sheep and cattle grazed. Two giant figures of Gog and Magog, carved in the turf in pre-historic times, were still being cleaned until the end of Elizabeth I's reign. A map from the time of the Civil War shows the presence of a windmill and it is here, in 1797, that the city's last local public execution took place.

The Hoe is also the site of Drake's famous game of bowls, played as the Spanish Armada advanced up the Channel. Plymouth was the base of the Elizabethan Navy and therefore a place of national importance. It was the threat posed by the Armada that made Drake realise the importance of defending it properly. In 1590, he petitioned the Queen to have a fort built on the Hoe, an area vital to the defence of the town as well as the ships in the Cattewater. She agreed and the result incorporated the existing waterside defences into a single fortification based on the angle bastion principle. This was subsequently overbuilt by The Royal Citadel.

Mount Batten

The peninsula opposite is Mount Batten, named after a parliamentary commander of Plymouth during the long siege of the Civil War. The tower, built about 60 years after Drake's Fort and shortly before the Royal Citadel, is an extremely rare example of a Commonwealth structure. Habitation of this site dates back to the Bronze Age. Later it was a Roman trading post and, for most of the last century, an R.A.F. seaplane base. Lawrence of Arabia was stationed there during the 1930s. For years it was off-limits but now the breakwater has been refurbished and marine developments and leisure activities have taken over the former military establishment. There's even a water-ferry link with The Mayflower Steps on the Barbican.

To the left, further up the River Plym, is Oreston which boasts a connection with Robinson Crusoe. He was, of course, Alexander Selkirk, found marooned on an uninhabited island and made famous in his own lifetime by Daniel Defoe's novel. We don't know how long Selkirk lodged at Oreston after his rescue but it was certainly long enough to court and marry his landlady in December 1720. A year and a day after the wedding, he died at sea, a victim of yellow fever.

Mount Batten Peninsula

The Royal Citadel

Plymouth was a distinctly Protestant town with a long history of opposition to Catholic Spain and the Inquisition. At the outbreak of the Civil War in 1642, Plymouth supported Cromwell and Parliament against Charles I and his Cavaliers, remaining Roundhead throughout the struggle even though Cornwall and most of the West Country were stoutly Royalist. It was a troublesome time for the town, which lay under siege for three years and four months. Its people endured great hardship. Food was scarce and the enemy cut Drake's Leat, causing severe shortage of water. When provisions were at their lowest, a large shoal of fish providentially entered Sutton Harbour in such numbers that it was possible to scoop them up in baskets (referred to as the Miracle of the Fishes).

The Royal Citadel

The most important battle took place in 1643. The King's forces made a surprise attack, advancing as far as Freedom Fields but, against heavy odds, the defenders managed to repel them. The battle is commemorated by a memorial in Freedom Park, at the crest of the hill where it was fought. Another reminder of the Civil War is Vapron Road in Mannamead, a corruption of 'Vapouring Hill', so called because of the smoke from the cannons that bombarded Plymouth. An estimated 4,000 people died as a result of that siege but Plymouth was never taken by the Royalists. In 1649, the King was eventually defeated and beheaded and, in 1653, Oliver Cromwell was made Lord Protector, governing England until his death 5 years later.

After 11 years, the monarchy was restored and Charles II returned to the throne in 1660. Believing the Navy 'vital to the safety, honour and welfare of the realm', he ordered the building of the Royal Citadel to protect the military and commercial harbour at Sutton Pool. He confiscated land belonging to the Corporation, offering no compensation whatsoever, and the foundation stone of this massive fortification was laid in 1666. Much of the building material was robbed from the walls of the old Plymouth Castle (see page 14).

Originally planned as a star-shaped fortress, it was adapted to incorporate the site of Drake's smaller, crumbling fort. Within its ramparts is a spacious Parade Ground surrounded by imposing buildings, an interesting collection of historic guns and a chapel. Because some of its cannons aimed towards the town, it was local belief that the Citadel had been built to watch over it as well as for wider military reasons – Plymouth had stood against the monarchy during the recent Civil War! Be this true or false, it is interesting to note that, until 1939, never a single shot had been fired in anger from these massive ramparts.

When Charles II died, he was succeeded by his brother James II. In 1688, only 3 years later, James fled the country and the governor of the Royal Citadel gave his support to William of Orange. Indeed, his declaration as King William III was actually read out here, the Citadel being the first English fortress to be commanded by him.

Gateway to the Citadel

The grand baroque gateway, attributed to Sir Thomas Fitz, once housed a drawbridge but that disappeared years ago. The niche is believed to have once held a statue of Charles II but today a garland of four large mortar rounds occupies this space.

In 1819 the Duke of Wellington was governor of the Royal Citadel before going on to becoming Prime Minister of England nine years later. Developments in armaments reduced the value of this type of fortification and, in 1888, the outer earthworks were landscaped and the perimeter ditch filled in. In 1936, further changes were made when the outer fortifications were pulled down to allow for Madeira Road to be built along the water's edge.

Since 1897, the Royal Citadel has been garrisoned by the Royal Artillery and, since 1962, has been home to 29 Commando Regiment. It has been in continuous military use ever since it was first built on the orders of Charles II.

Boer War Memorial

In 1652 the Dutch had colonised South Africa but, since this was a strategic position commanding the sea route to the east, Britain and France soon began to war over it. Britain eventually gained possession in 1814.

In the beginning the population remained mainly Boer (from Boeren which is Dutch for farmers) but British settlers soon began to arrive. In 1833 slavery was abolished in the British Empire and the Boers, who lost their slaves as a result, felt that they had been inadequately compensated. This resentment, combined with other grievances (mainly that of English being the official language) led to the trek north and the subsequent formation of the republics of the Transvaal and the Orange Free State. Their independence was recognised by Britain until the discovery of diamonds near the Orange River in 1867 and also, a few years later, the great diamond field at Kimberley. The area was immediately seized, even though the Boers had a better claim to it. Ten years later, the Transvaal was also taken. The opening of goldfields in this area led to an influx of British settlers who soon began to out-number the Boers. This stirred up even more animosity and finally war broke out in 1899. At first the Boers were stronger but volunteers soon arrived from Britain, which resulted in the famous reliefs of Mafeking and Ladysmith, the capture of their capitol Blomfontein and eventual British victory.

Boer War Memorial

Standing in a corner of The Hoe, within the shadow of the Royal Citadel, is the Boer War Memorial, an obelisk of red Swedish granite with four bronze plaques at its base, each containing scenes of various engagements of the Boer War (1899-1902). Above them is a flowing Greek wave, emblematic of the sea beyond which many of our soldiers died.

Alfred Mosely, a South African merchant of West Country descent, was too old to take part in the fighting so, instead, he financed a hospital and this memorial to the memory of the men of the Gloucester, Somerset and Devon Regiments who died in South Africa (including Christian Victor, Prince of Schleswig-Holstein, a grandson of Queen Victoria).

Royal Marines' Memorial

Detail from Boer War Memorial

Royal Marines' Memorial

This striking bronze statue, unveiled in 1921, is the Royal Marines' Memorial to their dead comrades. It depicts St. George slaying the eagle of militarism with the words 'So he passed over and all the trumpets sounded for him on the other side'. The limestone building to the right of the memorial is the world famous Marine Biological Association Laboratory. Plymouth was chosen because of the rich and varied fauna to be found here. Opened in 1888, it is one of the world's leading research stations. No fewer than seven Nobel Prize winners have carried out research there.

Plymouth Dome

An exciting addition to the Hoe is the award-winning Plymouth Dome, an all-weather attraction that is open throughout the year. This purpose-built centre, tucked into the cliff-side, has panoramic windows that provide a wonderful viewing point overlooking The Sound with text panels that explain the various points of interest around the bay.

It is a fascinating venue with a wide range of atmospheric constructions and interactive equipment that help explain this wonderful city from a geographical and historic viewpoint. The story of Plymouth unfolds before your eyes as you

Plymouth Dome

are taken on a voyage of discovery through 400 years of its history. Hear about Drake, Cook, Raleigh, the Pilgrim Fathers and the great engineers who built lighthouses on the Eddystone Rocks. The Climate Zone gives you a hands-on link to the Met Office and illustrates how the oceans affect our world and there is also a moving audio-visual account of Plymouth during the Blitz. You witness the Luftwaffe's devastation and, after the awful destruction, the determination of the people and the subsequent reconstruction of the City as it rose from the ashes.

Facilities include the Dolphin Café and an excellent gift shop full of all manner of things linked to Plymouth and the exhibition.

Jutting out into the sea immediately below Plymouth Dome is Tinside Lido, the recently refurbished art-deco swimming pool.

Tinside Pool

Plymouth Breakwater

Ships in Plymouth Sound had always been vulnerable to storms and a breakwater was sorely needed. In 1812 Sir John Rennie began work on an ambitious project to check the violence of the sea and thereby greatly enhance the use of the harbour. Work was delayed by the Napoleonic Wars but the project was finally completed in 1841. Rennie's breakwater changed what had been a treacherous bay into a place of safety.

This 4½ million ton structure of limestone and dovetailed granite blocks nearly equals the weight of the Great Pyramid. It stands

2½ miles offshore, some 80ft deep (25m), stretching almost one mile across the mouth of Plymouth Sound. On the western end is this white granite lighthouse and, on the eastern end, a 25ft high beacon topped by a hollow globe of gun metal, 6ft in diameter, designed to serve as a refuge for shipwrecked sailors.

The small fort in the centre is not actually a part of it but one of Palmerston's Follies, a ring of defensive forts built around Plymouth and Portsmouth in response to the French invasion scare of the late 1850s (see Crownhill Fort, page 26).

Plymouth Breakwater

Drake's Island

This small island covers about six acres and rises almost 100ft above sea level. In the 12th century it was in the hands of the Priors of Plympton and contained only a tiny chapel dedicated to St. Michael. Later, this chapel became dedicated to St. Nicholas, the patron saint of sailors, and the island then became known by the same name. In the mid 16th century, the chapel was

Drake's Island

demolished and defences built in its place. When Sir Francis Drake was appointed governor, about 1583, he greatly improved these defences and it became known as Drake's Island - the name it is known by to this day.

During the 17th century, after the restoration of the monarchy, it was used as a state prison to house some of the parliamentarians of the Civil War. During the World War I it was used as an arsenal and a network of tunnels was constructed for the storage of explosives.

On the right of the picture are the old premises of the old Royal Western Yacht Club where Sir Francis Chichester landed in 1967, on completion of the first single-handed circumnavigation of the world in Gypsy Moth IV.

However, Plymouth must have been a less welcome sight to another famous visitor - Napoleon Bonaparte. In 1815, after defeat by the Duke of Wellington at the Battle of Waterloo, he was brought to Plymouth Sound as a prisoner aboard the Bellerophon. She remained at anchor for several days, during which time little boats shuttled out so that local people could get a glimpse of Napoleon. It is said that he obliged by standing on deck and posing. A painting of this very scene hangs in Plymouth City

Art Gallery. He also posed for a portrait by Charles Eastlake (presently hanging in the National Maritime Museum) after which he sent the artist his cloak, complete with medals, to ensure that he got every detail absolutely correct. Soon afterwards, Napoleon was exiled to St. Helena where he died six years later.

Plymouth Pier

A 500ft long Victorian pier, constructed in 1884, once stood immediately in front of the Belvedere. Sadly this magnificent structure was one of the many victims of the blitz of World War II.

The Belvedere

The age of the steps and terraces that lead from Hoe Road up to the Promenade is uncertain but the pleasing Belvedere was constructed in 1891, the year of Queen Victoria's golden wedding jubilee.

Unfortunately, a camera obscura that had stood on this site had to be demolished to make way for it. The pillars of the two upper tiers are reputed to have come from an old Plymouth market. It is said that, from the sea, the Belvedere represents the Queen's wedding cake.

Immediately below The Belvedere is the site of the old Bull Ring. In the 17th century, animals were baited here by bulldogs, partly for sport and partly because it was believed to tenderise the meat. Indeed, butchers were obliged to do this by law. There is a record of one actually being fined for not complying. Today this site is a small garden of remembrance - a weeping willow surrounded by simple plaques commemorating regiments or specific battles. Unlike the other military memorials, this one is tiny and possibly more poignant for that.

The Belvedere

The Lighthouses

Winstanley designed the first Eddystone lighthouse which was built in 1698, fourteen miles out to sea, on one of the most treacherous reefs in the British Channel. It was the first offshore lighthouse in the world and, despite its ornate design, was a miracle of achievement. Its construction was interrupted by the French Wars, during which time Winstanley and his men were seized and imprisoned. They

were later released by Louis XIV for humanitarian reasons. One night in 1703, England experienced one of the worse storms ever recorded and, by the morning, there was no trace of the lighthouse nor its occupants. Strangely, a model of the structure, which was at Winstanley's home in Essex, hundreds of miles away, was also

Winstanley's Lighthouse

destroyed by the same storm. An accurate silver model, made around 1698, is on display at Plymouth City Museum.

In 1711, a second lighthouse was constructed by Rudyerd, using granite and wood, but this was destroyed by fire in 1755. During the fire, the lead cupola of the lighthouse began to melt and, as the lighthouse-keeper was looking up at it, he swallowed some of

Smeaton's Lighthouse in situ on the Eddystone Rocks

the molten metal. No one believed him until he died a few days later and the doctor produced a lump of solidified lead as the cause of death.

The third lighthouse, pictured left, has 93 steps. It was built by Smeaton in 1759 using interlocking stones that were laid in position on the grassy slopes of the Hoe before being transported out to the Eddystone Rocks from Millbay Harbour. This lighthouse stood for over 120 years, and was only removed in 1882 because a fault was detected in the rocks below. The structure was dismantled, stone by stone, and re-erected here on the Hoe in place of an old navigation beacon. Smeaton's design set the pattern for all later offshore lighthouses and its image appeared behind Britannia on the old bronze penny until the coin ceased to be minted in 1970.

The replica beacon standing nearby looks slightly out of place, but it is not. Beacons have stood on Plymouth Hoe since medieval times. They were well maintained and could only be lit on the orders of two J.P.s who, before doing so, would satisfy themselves of the need by sending trustees to the previous beacon to check.

The present lighthouse, designed by Sir James Douglas and lit in 1882, stands on a rock adjacent to the stump of Smeaton's tower. At night its regular, flashing light can be seen in the distance and, on a clear day, it is even visible with the naked eye, on the horizon, just right of the breakwater.

The Promenade

Military and naval parades still take place here overlooked by Drake's statue, the memorials and the elegant houses of Elliot Terrace that were built by John Pethick. This local builder, once Mayor of Plymouth and known to all as Honest John, was also responsible for building the present Guildhall. The splendid view from here would have been enjoyed by the 2nd Viscount Astor and his wife Nancy who used to live at 3, Elliot Terrace. They were Lord Mayor and Lady Mayoress of Plymouth during Word War II and through the early days of the city's reconstruction. In 1919, Lady Nancy Astor, a native of Virginia, became the first woman to take a seat in the House of Commons. She represented the Sutton district of Plymouth for 25 years.

Elliot Terrace

Military War Memorial

The bronze figure with wreath and sword at the top of Lockyer Street is the memorial to the military dead of both World Wars.

With the fall of France in 1940, Plymouth became an easy target for the German Air Force. On the evening of 20th March 1941, only two hours after the departure of the King and Queen, the City received a massive air attack, the first of many. The glow of the fires could be seen for miles and many fire engines dashed here to help on that terrible night, only to stand by helplessly because their equipment was unsuitable. This highlighted the need for uniformity of technique and equipment and, as a result, the National Fire Service was born. The following morning, Plymouth was unrecognizable. The Blitz continued for 7 nights and, during that week alone, over 1,000 civilians were killed. A communal funeral was held and the bodies buried in a mass grave.

Much of the ancient town centre was completely obliterated that year - shops and municipal buildings were either destroyed or rendered useless. During these devastating bomb raids more than 20,000 houses were destroyed or seriously damaged, mainly by fire. Not one single street escaped some damage. No words can convey the horror of the bombing. The Blitz took a terrible toll and Plymouth achieved the doubtful distinction of being the worst bombed city in Britain. 'Their homes were down but their hearts were high,' Churchill said of the survivors.

Military War Memorial

Naval War Memorial

Naval War Memorial

This, the tallest of the monuments on the Hoe, is identical to those at Chatham and Portsmouth. Erected about 1920, it was designed by Sir Robert Lorimer, who also designed the Scottish National War Memorial in Edinburgh. The Portland stone column has carved lions at its four corners and is surmounted by projecting carved ships' prows and statues representing the four winds that blow - angry north, fair south, cruel east and kindly west.

It is a memorial to Plymouth's naval dead of World War I who have no other grave but the sea. Later, a sunken garden was added to carry the bronze plaques that record the dead of World War II. Lists of the 22,443 names are available at the Central Library and from the Tourist Information Office.

On the second Sunday in November a remembrance service is held at this and thousands of other cenotaphs throughout the land, in memory of those who fought and died for their country ' Lest we forget'.

International Air Monument

Erected as recently as 1989 and long overdue, this bronze statue of an airman stands in tribute to the men and women of all countries who came to Britain to serve in the allied air forces during World War II.

International Air Monument

Statue of Sir Francis Drake

secured a victory over the heavy Spanish galleons, which they then pursued as far as the Firth of Forth in Scotland. Many of them sailed completely around the British Isles. The combined effect of weather and British action accounted for the loss of half the Spanish ships.

The Armada Memorial

Erected in 1888, on the 300th anniversary, this memorial overlooks Plymouth Sound where the epic battle began. The tall granite plinth, surmounted by bronze figures of Britannia and a lion, holds medallions and shields. At the base are cannons and cannon-ball piles, and a bronze relief depicting a scene from the battle. The pedestal is embellished with coasts of arms of those who took part and towns that contributed ships, as well as portraits of the admirals in charge of operations - Sir Francis Drake, John Hawkins, Lord Howard of Effingham and Lord Henry Seymour.

Anchor from HMS Ark Royal

In 1593 Drake represented Plymouth in Parliament but, three years later, this great explorer, privateer and scourge of the Spanish Armada died on board the Defiance. He was buried at sea in the Caribbean.

A walk down Armada Way will take you past this anchor of the aircraft carrier HMS Ark Royal - the same name as the flagship of the fleet against the Spanish Armada.

Sir Francis Drake

This bronze statue, erected in 1884, is of Sir Francis Drake, one of the greatest sailors the world has known. He was born about 1542 at Crowndale, Tavistock (15 miles from Plymouth) but spent most of his life on board ship helping to establish English supremacy at sea. In 1577 he set off in The Pelican, later re-named The Golden Hind, to become the first Englishman to encompass the globe, battling with the Spaniards en-route and greatly injuring their pride. This was only the second ever circumnavigation, and established him as a great navigator. Other ships of the squadron were lost or returned home and his own was several times given up for lost. The journey, which had taken almost three years, led to the formation of the East India Company and much else besides.

Drake, a privateer who revelled in plundering Spanish ships and ports in South America, became a great favourite of Elizabeth I and was knighted on board his ship at Deptford. His successes brought great wealth to the Queen and also allowed him to buy Buckland Abbey as his home (see page 29).

He became mayor of Plymouth and began work on the 14-mile long leat which was to bring the first fresh water supply to the town from the River Meavy on Dartmoor. Plymouth became the first town in Britain to bring a regular water supply from outside her boundaries and this was in use for the next 300 years. It was about this time that he encouraged the defence of Drake's Island.

Tension between Spain and England was growing and war finally broke out in 1585. Drake commanded the fleet, which he took to the Spanish Main (Central America) inflicting great damage. In 1587 he attacked the Spanish fleet that had collected in the Bay of Cadiz, destroying many ships. This impudent act, know as the 'singeing of the King of Spain's beard', succeeded in delaying the Spanish attack. The vast Armada of 160 ships and 20,000 men did eventually set sail in 1588.

The Queen did not entirely trust Drake (he didn't always do as he was told) so she put him second in command to Lord Howard and together they set out with the English fleet that had lain in wait in Plymouth's Cattewater. Their daring tactics in lighter ships soon

Armada Memorial

Plymouth Pavilions

This facility is open 364 days a year and fully accessible to the disabled. It consists of three inter-connecting rotunda which offer a variety of excellent venues, the largest of these being the Arena, a versatile event hall capable of hosting everything from banquets, conferences, exhibitions and international sporting events, to a full programme of pop and rock music, light entertainment and orchestral concerts. It can accommodate up to 4,000 people and the very latest technology offers infinitely flexible facilities for all events. The complex also contains an ice rink and an imaginative swimming pool with waves, waterfalls, marooned galleon and a beach, as well as delightful water slides, one of which whizzes you outside the building. Other amenities include bars, bistro, snack bar and cafeteria.

Plymouth Pavilions

Derry's Clock

This picture shows three contrasting styles of architecture. In the foreground is Derry's Clock, one of the few pre-war structures still standing in its original position, having survived the blitz when all around it lay in ruins. Today it is almost hidden behind the Theatre Royal but, originally, this tower occupied a prominent position on a busting junction with many of the old city streets radiating from it. Derry's Clock was always a conspicuous landmark and a favourite meeting place for lovers and, as such, is of great sentimental value.

William Derry, who was mayor three times between 1861 and 1880, commissioned the clock in commemoration of the wedding of the Prince of Wales in 1862. Because rates money could not lawfully be spent on a clock, there was great controversy over the cost. However, since a fountain was permitted, the tower was built with stone basins although it never held water, and never could - a dry sense of humour. The clock is sometimes called the Four Faced Deceiver because it appears to show different times unless read straight on, the reason being that the hands stand 3 inches away from the face.

Behind the tower is The Bank, a distinctive building of rusticated ashlar that is very pleasing to the eye. It was once the Devon and Dorset Bank but is now an attractive public house.

In the background is The Civic Centre, a 14 storey building that was opened in 1962 by the Queen and Prince Philip. Adjoining it is the Council Chamber where items on display include maces, civic plate, glass engravings, antiquarian prints, paintings and historic city records. The building stands in Royal Parade.

After 4 years of air raids during the Second World War, there had been such awful destruction that Plymouth was faced with a massive rebuilding problem. It could have been rebuilt along the lines of the pre-blitzed city which would have been mainly financed by the War Damage Commission but this alternative was rejected in favour of Professor Abercombie's 'Plan for Plymouth'. His idea was to take advantage of the devastation to build an entirely new city centre.

Reconstruction began with the opening of Royal Parade, the first main thoroughfare, simply a road of concrete amidst rubble and demolition work but an inspiring sight to the inhabitants of Plymouth. In 1947, it was officially opened by King George VI and Queen Elizabeth. The city had become the first in Britain to rise from its ashes.

Derry's Clock

HALLS PLYMPTON BREWERY CO

City Maces

The Theatre Royal

The old Theatre Royal, built by John Foulston in 1811, was an elegant building that stood, together with the Royal Hotel, at the corner of Lockyer Street. It was demolished in 1937, leaving the City almost devoid of live entertainment facilities. Post-war attempts to fill that void proved unsatisfactory and a debate began on whether or not to build a theatre that would be good enough to be the main touring venue for the South West.

By 1974, a major development project was designed which included a new Theatre Royal near the site of its predecessor. However, the changing economic climate put an end to all but the theatre itself. Construction finally began on the rocky western corner of Royal Parade in 1979, and was completed three years later.

Theatre Royal

The result of this imaginative project, containing two theatres, is unique in both design and construction. Indeed, the main auditorium has one of the biggest stages in the country. A major feature of the design incorporates a section of the ceiling that can be lowered to cut off the upper circle, thereby reducing the seating capacity from 1,296 to 768 and creating a more intimate atmosphere. Other interesting features include a front of stage that can be lowered to form an orchestra pit capable of seating 76 musicians, and an assisted resonance system which can be altered to give the sound conditions best suited to the show in progress, be it a solo or a massed brass band. As well as, from time to time, being the regional home of the Royal Shakespeare Company and the Royal National Theatre, the Theatre Royal frequently creates shows prior to a West-End run

The second auditorium is a small, flexible studio theatre known as The Drum. It can seat about 200 people, dependant on format. It has movable seating that can be pre-arranged in various forms to provide exciting arrangements such as 'theatre in the round'. It contains its own dressing rooms and wardrobe facilities, making it quite independent of the main auditorium.

The theatre was built by Plymouth City Council with contributions from the E.E.C. Regional Development fund and the Arts Council of Great Britain. Since it is open to the public, visitors may wander through the three spacious foyers to view an exhibition or simply sit and watch the world go by through the tinted glass wall that overlooks Royal Parade. The Circle Café offers a wide and varied menu prior to many performances whilst the Stalls Coffee Bar is open all day on show days serving drinks and light snacks. In both The Drum and the Theatre Royal due consideration has been given to disabled persons.

The pedestrianisation of the City centre has transformed the shopping area, providing seating among plants and shrubs, play areas for children, a massive sundial and a circle of stones for open-air theatre.

Royal Hotel

Theatre auditorium

The Guildhall

Shortly after receipt of the town charter in 1439, a medieval Town Guildhall was built in Plymouth. That was demolished and replaced in 1606 by a fine Jacobean guildhall that used to stand in High Street, near St. Andrew's Church. That was an imposing, colonnaded structure with a clock tower and a room above for the mayor, magistrates and councillors. At one end stood the notorious clink (prison) with its two dungeons. This whole magnificent structure cost just £794 to build. A market used to be held around its granite pillars and, it is commonly believed, these pillars today form part of the Belvedere on the Hoe. This Jacobean guildhall remained until 1800, when a Regency guildhall designed by Eveleigh was erected but that 'Old Guildhall' was found to be quite unsatisfactory for its purpose and therefore served

Plymouth Guildhall

for only 70 years. The building itself was converted into the Free Library and stood until 1941, when it became yet another victim of the Blitz.

The present site was chosen in 1870 and work began in that year on the New Guildhall, pictured here. Although reduced to a shell during the Blitz, it was extensively renovated. The Gothic exterior with its 13th century French influence was retained, the beautiful stone relief carvings of the exterior north wall facing Royal Parade being part of that original Victorian decor. These panels extol the virtues of Commerce, Religion, the Arts and Sciences.

In 1959, the Guildhall was re-opened by Field Marshall The Viscount Montgomery of Alamein. Its interior and entrance are

Stone relief carvings on Guildhall

Chandeliers in the Guildhall

entirely new, the foyer containing a model of Plymouth as it was in 1620. The sculptured ceiling panels of the Twelve Labours of Hercules are the work of Plymouth sculptor David Weekes and the three huge chandeliers, each weighing about half a ton, represent the three old towns of Devonport, Stonehouse and Plymouth which amalgamated to form the present City. Depicted in the set of 14 magnificent stained glass windows are some of Plymouth's most notable historical events from as long ago as the Black Prince's French expedition and the Breton raids, to the more recent enemy attacks of the last war and the City's subsequent reconstruction. It also contains a rare Gobelin-stitch tapestry that is over 100 years old, the work of Flemish weavers and a gift from Napoleon III to Lord Clarendon (kindly on loan to the city from the present Lord Clarendon). Its subject, The Miraculous Draught of Fishes after a drawing by Raphael, is of particular significance to the city because, during the siege of Plymouth in the Civil War, a shoal of pilchards appeared in Sutton Harbour, like a miracle to the starving inhabitants.

Charles Church

The shell of Charles Church is a prominent landmark and an outstanding example of 17th century Gothic architecture. When Charles I installed a cleric who strongly supported him at nearby St. Andrew's Church, the Corporation of Plymouth, anxious to protect its hard-won independence from Royal intervention, applied to the King for a new parish to be created on the pretext that St. Andrew's was not large enough for the religious needs of the community. Hoping to persuade him, the name of Charles was suggested for the new church, with the result that he could hardly refuse.

Work began in 1640 but was interrupted by the Civil War, during which time Plymouth, which supported Parliament, was blockaded by Royalist forces for three long years. The church was eventually completed in 1658 although a wooden spire was not added until 50 years later. This was replaced by the stone spire in 1767.

Time seems to have stood still for Charles Church since that fateful day in 1941 when it was gutted by German Bombs. Today, its shell stands as a memorial to the city's civilian casualties of the Second World War - 1,172 people killed and 3,269 significantly injured. These terrible statistics do not include service casualties.

Plymouth City Museum & Art Gallery

These square hewn stone buildings are the Plymouth City Museum & Art Gallery and the Central Library that were opened in 1910. The library was completely gutted during the Blitz and later rebuilt behind its original façade. The museum building was more fortunate and survived intact.

Today it houses a splendid collection of fine and decorative art with paintings, drawings etc by Plymouth artist such as Sir Joshua Reynolds, James Northcote, Sir Charles Lock Eastlake, Samuel Prout, B.R.Haydon and works by members of the Newlyn School. It also includes the 18th century Cottonian Collection with drawings, prints, bronzes, a library sculpture and relics relating to Sir Joshua Reynolds. There is a wonderful ceramics collection that, of course, includes Plymouth Porcelain by Cookworthy, the first person in Britain to produce hard past porcelain successfully, as well as other items that represent the local history of Plymouth, including its maritime history. The museum also houses a fascinating selection of archaeological material from Dartmoor and the region, and a natural history collection, recently re-displayed, that includes many minerals from the South West as well as a fine herbarium collection.

On the other side of the road stands the University of Plymouth. It has an excellent reputation academically, in research and for its range of services to industry and works closely with its partner colleges, one of which, Plymouth College of Art and Design, stands just below the museum whilst another, Plymouth College of Further Education, can be found a little further afield at Devonport.

Shell of Charles Church

Plymouth/Cookworthy porcelain

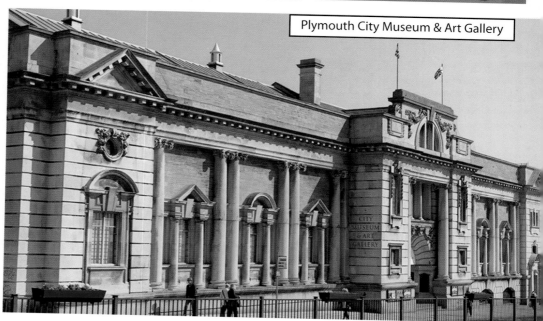

Plymouth City Museum & Art Gallery

South Yard, Devonport Royal Dockyard

provide three covered all-weather docks and, in 1980, the nuclear submarine refit complex was built on what had been the coaling station. In 1987 the dockyard was privatised and is now run by D.M.L. It lost much of its workforce in the process but major redevelopment that followed made it the only base for refitting the U.K.'s latest Vanguard class nuclear-powered submarines.

During World War II, despite sustaining considerable damage, the dockyard continued to fulfil its vital function and, during the Falklands conflict of 1982, mindful of the yard's vital role in support of the Royal Navy, the workforce worked around the clock to fulfil its obligations.

Plymouth is also home to the Royal William Victualling Yard at Stonehouse, completed in 1835. Around the basin are beautiful buildings that once contained a brewhouse, cooperage, slaughterhouse, mills and a bakery to provide for the Royal Navy. By the turn of the century, victualling needs had changed. By the 1950s, the yard was virtually obsolete and used as a base for the amphibious assault marines 539 squadron before transferring to Turnchapel in the 1990s. These buildings are some of Plymouth's most impressive and, since 1993, there has been a programme to prepare them for new uses.

Devonport Royal Dockyard

This is situated in the Hamoaze, on the eastern banks of the River Tamar, which provides a magnificent anchorage with a deep-water channel to the sea. The original 15-acre has expanded to the present area of over 900 acres, making Devonport the principal Royal Navy Yard and the biggest dockyard in Western Europe. For hundreds of years Plymouth has played a key role in sea defence. From before Tudor times there had been considerable commercial and naval shipbuilding and repairs around the Cattewater area but it was the French Navy's activity at the western end of the English Channel that prompted the need for a dockyard here. Since there was no remaining location to accommodate it in the Plym estuary, the Tamar estuary was chosen. Work began in 1690 upon the orders of William of Orange (William III), his choice of Plymouth probably influenced by the support he'd received from the town when he overthrew James II.

The new town that grew up around the Dockyard became known as Dock. Whilst the old town of Plymouth remained prosperous, Dock began to grow until, by the 18th century, it became larger than Plymouth itself. In 1824, George IV changed its name to Devonport and the 125ft Devonport Column was built to celebrate this event. The dockyard expanded rapidly. In 1844, the need for steam ship facilities led to a major extension of the yard at Keyham and, in 1896, North Yard was added to deal with the huge dreadnoughts. In 1975, Keyham Steam Yard was redeveloped to

Crownhill Fort

This is one of Palmerston's Follies, a ring of defensive forts built in response to the French invasion scare of the late 1850s. Lord Palmerston was the Prime Minister responsible for their construction and his name became immortalised as a result. They rather unfairly acquired the name follies because they were expensive and never used but, had there been a French invasion, he would have been the hero of the hour. Plymouth's forts stretched from Staddon Heights to Whitsand Bay, the largest and most important being Crownhill Fort, Plymouth's best-kept secret. It is so well hidden that people hardly notice it, and that was exactly the intention when it was built. It may look like a wooded hill but it is actually a cunningly concealed fortress surrounded by a 30ft dry ditch dug by hand from solid rock. The entrance is via a handsome Norman arch, a theme repeated throughout the building. Since British expertise lay in the building of coastal defences, its design was based on the European model of land fortresses, which explains the use of French terminology. It took 9 years to build, with 4 fighting levels, 32 gun positions (many with working cannon), 350 rifle loops, stables, artillery stores, barracks for 300 men, massive parade ground and the only operational Moncrieff in the world, a disappearing gun that's still fired on selected weekends.

It was retained by the army for over a century - during World War I as a recruitment and transit depot for troops, in World War II as an anti-aircraft battery and, during the Falklands conflict of 1982, as an assembly point. In 1986, surplus to M.O.D requirements, it was acquired by the charity Landmark Trust and underwent much needed restoration work. Today this impressive fort, the only one to survive unaltered, is open to the public. Children love the unrestricted access to its massive earth ramparts, hidden gun emplacements, rifle galleries and rabbit warren of passages and tunnels. Crownhill Fort is the sort of place that, once discovered, you do not forget in a hurry.

Crownhill Fort

River Tamar Crossings

Since Victorian times, the River Tamar has been the border between Devon and Cornwall. Before that, Millbrook to Cawsand was part of Devon. In the middle ages, the only links from Plymouth to Cornwall were ferry crossings to Cremyll and Saltash. The growth of the Dockyard made it necessary to open a third crossing to Torpoint in 1791 (today a vehicle ferry). The Saltash crossing has been replaced by two suspension bridges. Plymouth had been connected by rail to London since 1848 and, in 1859, the Royal Albert Railway Bridge was opened by Prince Albert. Still in use and largely unchanged, this single-track railroad, suspended on massive chains below arched wrought iron tubes was the last and greatest railway work of Isambard Kingdom Brunel, a gifted engineer, one of the most famous of his day. He had a strong influence on Plymouth, his mother's birthplace, and played a large part in bringing it into the Rail Age. The Tamar Road Bridge, opened in 1962 by the late Queen Mother, has a total span of 1,848ft. and clearance of 110ft., and provides the main road link with Cornwall. In 1999, whilst undergoing necessary strengthening work, 2 extra lanes were added. A pedestrian ferry still operates to Cremyll from Admiral's Hard in Stonehouse. This is the beginning of the Waterfront Walk, a footpath that stretches around the Hoe, through the Barbican, past Cattedown, Plymstock and Oreston, around Mount Batten and as far as Jennycliff.

Tamar Bridges

Robert Falcon Scott Memorial

At Mount Wise, overlooking the River Tamar as it enters the sea, stands this magnificent bronze group depicting Courage supported by Devotion and crowned by Immortality. Below, in bronze relief, are poignant scenes of the expedition and portraits of Scott, Oates, Wilson, Bowers and Evans surrounded by Scott's moving words: 'Had I lived I should have had a tale to tell of the hardship, endurance and courage of my companions which would have stirred the heart of every Englishman'.

Scott was born in Plymouth in 1868 and, by 1900, become a Commander in the Royal Navy. His bid to be the first to reach the South Pole was the last of the old-style adventures but it also had a serious scientific purpose. His rival, a Norwegian named Amundsen, relied on dogs for transport and food but Scott's refusal to do the same meant that his team had to footslog the last 150 miles. They arrived on 17th January 1912, one month after his rival. Scott summed up their feelings in his diary: 'Great God, this is an awful place and terrible enough for us to have laboured to it without the reward of priority'. The Norwegian returned before winter set in but the 800-mile round journey, dreadful weather and lack of food proved too much for Scott's team. They died just 11miles from stores that might have saved their lives.

Scott Memorial

Mount Edgcumbe House

Nestling amongst trees on the opposite bank of the River Tamar is the red sandstone Tudor Mansion of the Edgcumbe family. Built in 1547, it was restored by the 6th Earl after extensive damage caused by the Blitz. Though it now stands in magnificent parkland with superb views, it was not always so. The 1779 sighting of the French and Spanish fleets caused a scare that resulted in the felling of trees bordering the shore to prevent unobserved landings by the enemy. The English, French and Italian gardens, laid out in the early 19th century, replace those wilderness gardens. The Italian has an 18th century Orangery that offers refreshments. The Rose Garden is a newer addition, as are the New Zealand and American Gardens which contain flora native to those countries, the connection being that recent Edgcumbes have lived in New Zealand, and American G.I.s were stationed here, embarking from Barn Pool in June 1944 for the 'D-Day' landings. In 2002, a new garden was created to celebrate the Queen's Golden Jubilee.

Mount Edgcumbe Country Park can be reached by taking Cremyll Pedestrian Ferry from Admiral's Hard or driving via Torpoint. The house, furnished with Edgcumbe family possessions in 18th century décor, has a small entrance fee but visitors may wander free of charge through the Grade I listed gardens, famous since the 18th century and once admired by no less than Queen Victoria herself. There are 865 acres of beautiful woodland and countryside to enjoy with more than 10 miles of coastline footpath, past Kingsand, Cawsand, Penlee Point, Rame Head and as far as Whitsand Bay. There's also an an 18th century gothic folly, an ancient Blockhouse, Victorian gun-emplacements, wild fallow deer and the national camellia collection...or you could seek out one of the seats or small buildings that have been deliberately placed to create views and moods and just enjoy the magic.

Mount Edgcumbe

Cotehele House

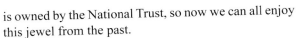

is owned by the National Trust, so now we can all enjoy this jewel from the past.

The house itself is utterly charming and the grounds are full of quiet little places. The garden provides a romantic setting for this ancient house, plunging down a valley towards the River Tamar whilst offering views towards Dartmoor in the distance. There is an overall sense of informality, with strong seasonal characteristics, and the range of plants mean that there is something to enjoy all year round. There are gardens on several levels, a lily-pond, a mediaeval dovecote, a fishpond and a winding path that leads down through the valley garden to the river's edge. The tiny chapel on the cliff was allegedly built in 1485 by Richard Edgcumbe, to give thanks for his deliverance - this is the spot where he hid after cleverly throwing his hat into the water so that his enemies would think he had drowned.

Cotehele House

This delightful medieval house of grey granite stands on the wooded banks of the River Tamar near Calstock in Cornwall. It is only a short journey from Plymouth and can be reached by road, rail or river.

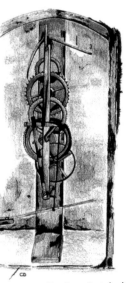

The Clock at Cotehele

It was rebuilt between 1485 and 1560, and internally remodelled in the 1650s. It was the home of the Edgcumbe family until Mount Edgcumbe became their main residence (see previous page) at which time Cotehele was relegated to a weekend and holiday retreat. For that reason it escaped renovation. Even the furnishings remained largely undisturbed - 17th century tapestries, needlework, period furniture, armour and a pre-pendulum clock (circa 1500) which is the earliest domestic clock of its type in England that is still unaltered and in its original position. Time here stands still. The main showrooms of the house have no artificial light and natural light levels are controlled. The darkness helped to preserve its treasures. Today the property

A stroll down-river will take you to the quayside where the restored Tamar sailing barge Shamrock is berthed alongside picturesque 18th and 19th century buildings (one of which contains a small shipping museum). From there, a short walk brings you to Cotehele Mill, which has been restored to working condition and now produces flour for sale. The adjoining buildings contain tools laid out as workshops - wheelwrights, carpenters, saddlers and blacksmith.

The Dovecote

Antony House

This house, also in Cornwall, stands five miles west of Plymouth via the Torpoint car ferry. There has been a house at Antony since the 14th century, and probably before, but the present one was built between 1711 and 1721 by Sir William Carew. It stands in a splendid park beside the River Lynher at a point which once commanded a medieval ferry crossing. The central block of the house is of silver-grey Pentewan stone and the wings, linked to the house by colonnades, are of red brick. The rooms are elegantly panelled and contain fine furniture and family portraits.

Antony House

The Bath Pond House, half a mile away beside the river estuary, was built in 1784. In 1847, upon the birth of his daughter, William Henry Pole-Carew built the schoolhouse and sanctuary at Maryfield and, in 1866, the nearby church to commemorate the birth of his son.

The Carew family came to Antony in the late 15th century, long before the present house was built, but the property had previously been associated with the great dynasties of medieval Cornwall. The family history is fascinating with great divisions and tragedies caused by the Civil War. John Carew, one of the judges at Charles I's trial, was executed in 1660 after the restoration of the monarchy whilst his brother, Sir Alexander, had been beheaded in 1644 on suspicion of helping the Royalists.

Antony was given to the National Trust by Sir John Carew Pole in 1961. The house continues to be the home of his son Richard and his family. The fact that it is still very much lived in adds greatly to its charm and interest.

Saltram House

Saltram stands on the southern banks of the River Plym, near Marsh Mills roundabout on the outskirts of Plymouth. This elegant George II mansion embodies the remains of a Tudor and a late Stuart house and was once the home of the Parker family. It is the largest country house in Devon and far outshines its Plymouth neighbours. Today the public has the good fortune to be able to wander through the gardens which contain an orangery and other fine buildings, visit the art gallery in the chapel or enjoy a tour of the house itself (it was used as a location for the film Sense and Sensibility).

Saltram House can be seen complete with its original furniture and paintings, many of which are by Sir Joshua Reynolds who was born at nearby Plympton. The magnificent dining room and saloon by Robert Adam has superb plasterwork and decoration dating from the 1780s. Although the delightful Georgian kitchen contains many items of great interest, the present day refreshments are prepared nearby, in more modest surroundings, by the National Trust that owns and cares for this superb building.

Saltram House

Buckland Abbey

This Abbey lies about nine miles north of Plymouth, in a secluded spot near Buckland Monachorum. It was built in 1278 by monks of the Cistercian order and is the most westerly of their monasteries. In addition to its religious duties, the Abbey also played an important economic and social role. Indeed, it was the source of livelihood for many of the local inhabitants. Consequently, when Henry VIII dissolved the monasteries in 1539, it caused great hardship to the villagers.

The property was bought by a Sir Richard Grenville but it was not until his famous grandson of the same name inherited it that it was converted into a country mansion.

When Sir Francis Drake returned, triumphant and rich from his circumnavigation of the world, he invested his money in property and decided to buy Buckland Abbey but, knowing that Grenville resented his success and the high regard he received from the Queen, he arranged for a kinsman to buy it in his stead for the generous sum of £3,400.

Drake died in 1596 and bequeathed his estates to his brother Thomas but they were confiscated during the Civil War by a leader of the Royalists, one 'Skellum' Grenville. However, the Grenville's return to the Abbey was short lived because, with the defeat of the King, it was returned to the Drakes and remained in the possession of the family until 1946.

Today Buckland Abbey is owned by the National Trust and presented in association with Plymouth City Museum whose collections provide many of the items on display. There is an interesting exhibition on the Life of the Abbey, including a film on the life of Drake, as well as some Drake relics - portraits, banners, a Silver Gilt Cup engraved with a map of the world as it was known at the time (an appropriate possession for a circumnavigator) and the famous Drake's

Drum. This drum was greatly treasured by Drake. Legend says it accompanied him as he circumnavigated the world and was at his side when he died. Afterwards, it was brought back to Buckland Abbey and accorded a place of honour in the Great Hall. The drum has a mystical quality. It is said to sound of its own accord when England is in danger, to rouse the spirit of Drake. It was reported to be clearly heard in 1914... and again in 1939.

Drake's Prayer

There must be a beginning of any great matter,
But the continuing unto the end,
Until it be thoroughly finished,
Yields the True Glory

In the pleasant grounds there are woodland walks, a herb garden, and a 150ft. tithe barn that was once used to house tithes collected from Abbey lands. This barn boasts a fine 15th century oak-beamed roof of exceptional span.

Drake's Drum

Buckland Abbey

Widgery Cross on Brat Tor

Hound of the Baskervilles, but today it is enjoyed by many millions of visitors. As well as the 500 miles (805 km) of footpaths and bridleways, there are two main roads that pass through open moorland and cross at Two Bridges (for information on the Transmoor Link bus telephone 0870.6082608). However, be wary; this peaceful, unspoilt wilderness can alter dramatically with a change in the uncertain weather that prevails there. Part of the northern moor is used by the Ministry of Defence for military training. Live firing takes place on a limited number of days each year but this is usually outside of the main visitor season and the range boundaries are well marked by red flags or red lanterns (for information on firing times telephone 0800.4584868).

Dartmoor National Park

Covering 368 square miles (954 sq. km), Dartmoor is an area of great beauty and rugged grandeur that lies to the north of Plymouth, in the very heart of Devon. Today it mainly consists of two high, boggy plateaux divided by the River Dart and its tributaries, but many millions of years ago it was part of a sea floor containing volcanic islands. About 290 million years ago the land folded, forming a mountain range beneath which lay the large masses of molten granite that pushed up to form the tors that are so characteristic of Dartmoor (Tor is the Celtic word for tower). Their strange shapes have evolved through thousands of years of weathering.

Today Dartmoor is the largest open space in South West England; a land of heather, bracken and gorse; of boggy hillsides, drystone walls and granite tors; of open moorland where sheep and cattle graze, and herds of ponies roam free; a place that is rocky and peat-bound where rushes and lichen and mosses thrive; a place of strong winds, high rainfall and swirling mists that is always exhilarating. The openness of its landscape gives a wonderful feeling of freedom and, around the fringes, are areas of enclosed farmland with small hamlets, villages and towns that are a joy to visit. Not so very long ago Dartmoor was regarded as a wild and savage place, a perfect setting for Sherlock Holmes and his

Spinsters Rock

An excursion to Dartmoor can offer far more than just tranquillity and beautiful scenery, for it contains several thousand sites of historical interest, including the remains of some of the oldest buildings in England. Here a pile of stones is rarely just a pile of stones! Ruins of Bronze Age huts, enclosures, burial monuments, stone circles and ritualistic stone rows are found in greater numbers here than anywhere else in Europe, making it one of the most important archaeological landscapes in Britain.

The first real evidence of occupation lies in the presence of flint tools belonging to the hunter-gatherers of the Middle Stone Age (Mesolithic: circa 8,000-4,000BC). At this time Dartmoor was largely covered with trees, but Mesolithic peoples were beginning to create clearings in the forest cover to attract grazing animals.

By 4,000 BC, the climate was warmer than it is now and a more settled way of life emerged. New Stone Age people (Neolithic) created farms, grew cereals and began to domesticate animals. Today all that remains of this period, apart from flint tools, are the stone-built *burial chambers*.

Around 2,000 BC, the period covering the transition from the Neolithic to the Bronze Age, the Beaker Folk dominated the area. They were so-called because of the distinctive pottery found in their graves. Although the acid soil has destroyed organic material such as bone or wood, there is still an abundance of hard evidence from this period including the impressive *stone rows* of which some 70 still survive, varying in length from 32 metres to 3.4 kilometres. Some are formed of a single line of stones and others have two parallel rows. Their function is unclear but their frequent association with burial sites suggests a ceremonial or religious purpose. It has also been suggested that they were used to study celestial bodies. As well as the *stone rows*, there are some 33 *stone circles* (upright stones enclosing areas of open ground), *menhirs* (single standing stones up to 3 metres in height), and *cairns* or *barrows* (burial mounds over the remains of important people). Over 350 *cairns* remain but it is highly probably that others have been dismantled to build the stonewalls. There are also about 100 *cists* or *kistvaens* (literally meaning stone chest), box-like structures made of granite slabs topped with a capstone and set into the ground for burial of a body or cremated ashes. When excavated, some prehistoric burial sites produced flint tools and pottery, suggesting a belief in an after-life.

White Moor Stone Circle and Outlier

Part of the Stone Row at Merrivale

From later in the Bronze Age (c.1,700-600BC) comes evidence of widespread occupation - over 25,000 acres of field systems bounded by low stony banks called *reaves* as well as remains of more that 5,000 round stone houses, often called *hut circles*. These Bronze Age dwellings vary in diameter from 3-10 metres and would originally have had a central pole supporting a conical roof made of wood covered with turf, heather or straw, usually in village groups scattered over a hillside and sometimes surrounded by an enclosure wall. Remains of *pounds* and *hut circles* are sometimes found at medieval sites, indicating the possibility of continuous occupation.

In the Bronze Age, the climate was warmer and dryer than today but, by about 500 BC, climatic changes made the moor a less pleasant place to live. The weather became colder and wetter so people gradually moved to lower ground and left high Dartmoor virtually deserted.

During the Iron Age (c.500 BC until the arrival of the Romans in the first century AD) Celts began to arrive in Britain. Evidence suggests that society became more aggressive and tribal. *Hillforts* were built in prominent locations to retreat into when under attack from raiding neighbours. About a dozen of these hilltop defences still exist on the moorland fringes but, since the structures were mostly of wood, only earthworks remain (Hembury Fort, with its deep ditches and high ramparts, is a fine example of an Iron Age Settlement).

From the 8th century onwards the climate began to improve again and people moved back up onto the moor, draining and clearing the swampy valleys and creating new farmland and settlements. The Domesday Book of 1086 shows 4,000-5,000 people living

Down Tor Stone Row

on Dartmoor. Their dwellings, in which humans and animals lived under the same roof, were *longhouses* made of stone and rectangular in shape. Almost all the churches and many of the bridges are medieval, as are the ruined castles at Okehampton and Lydford. The latter was an important Saxon borough and the site of a mint. Coins minted there (*Danegeld*) were used to buy off the Vikings with the result that far more can now be found in Scandinavian museums than in this country. Until the 19th century Lydford was the administrative centre for Dartmoor...and much feared for its 'severe justice'.

During the climatic shift of the early 1300s, Dartmoor became much wetter, making farming more difficult. This, together with the population shrinkage that resulted from the Black Death (1348-50), meant that some farms and villages were deserted as people once again abandoned Dartmoor for the more hospitable lower ground.

The Little Ice Age (c.1550-1700) produced the coldest climate since the last Ice Age. It did not warm up again until the Napoleonic Wars, which was rather fortunate because, in the late 18th century, work began on Dartmoor Prison, built to house prisoners from the wars with France and America - and Princetown is the highest village on the moor! As well as the prison, it's also home to Dartmoor National Park Authority's 'High Moorland Visitor Centre' that is open all year.

The 1900s was the age of mineral extraction (lead, zinc, silver and copper) and of the china clay industry, which is now the area's most important mineral resource. Remnants can still be seen of these and other industries such as gunpowder, glass, paper, ice making and quarrying. Granite from Haytor Quarry was used to build Buckingham Palace, Covent Garden, The British Museum and the National Gallery. The corbels of the old London Bridge (now in America) came from Foggintor Quarry.

The harsh climate means that there are few trees on the high moor and those that do grow are twisted and shaped by the wind. Many of the river valleys and lower slopes are covered by ancient semi-natural upland oak woods. Only hardy breeds of livestock survive. Ponies, which are an integral part of the moorland landscape and help to give Dartmoor its unique character, date back to around 2,000 BC. In the past they have been invaluable as pack animals as well as cart-pullers, but today they live in herds and enjoy a more leisurely existence. Although they live out all year round, they're not wild but they are untamed, so be careful.

Dartmoor certainly receives its fair share of rainfall - Princetown receives 5 times more rain than Exeter. The peat ground acts like a gigantic sponge, holding vast amounts of rainwater and then releasing it slowly. It is the source of most of Devon's rivers and, since most towns get their water from one of its 8 reservoirs, it is one of the South West's most important sources of water. Drake's famous leat, 14 miles long (22km), brought fresh water to Plymouth from Headweir which now forms part of Burrator Reservoir, and the Devonport leat, 24 miles long (39km), drew from three different sources near Princetown. Separate leats were necessary owing to conflict between the two towns but, ironically, Devonport leat now adds more than a million gallons per day to Plymouth's water supply.

Horn's Cross

The first roads would originally have connected one farming settlement to another but, by the 12th century, they had become the main routes linking the scattered towns. There would also have been trading and other routes across the moor. Important amongst the ancient trackways and pathways are the Abbots Way (granite crosses marking the safe track across the southern moor - used by people travelling between the Abbeys of Buckland, Tavistock and Buckfast) and the Lichway (literally meaning the way of the dead, lich is the Saxon word for corpse - the route along which corpses were carried across the moor for burial at Lydford). Burials, baptisms, weddings etc. had to take place at the parish church and, since much of Dartmoor lay within the Parish of Lydford (the largest in Britain), bodies from as far as Babeny had to be carried 8 miles (13 km) in fine weather, increasing to 12 miles (19 km) in bad! However, in 1260 the Bishop of Exeter granted dispensation for all sacraments to be held at nearby Widecombe church. There

are many eery tales surrounding the ancient Lichway. Both these ancient routes cross rivers either by ford, stepping stones or clapper bridge, large slabs of granite supported on stone piers, the most plentiful material since there were few trees here. There is an excellent example at Postbridge. The more recent tramways and railways were built to carry stone, tin and peat off the moor.

In earlier centuries there were four main industries on Dartmoor - farming, tinning, stone working and the cloth trade. Apart from farming, these have almost died out. Since tin is essential for the production of bronze, it is probable that the tin industry existed in the Bronze Age, but the earliest recorded activity is in the 12th century. This was streaming, the taking of alluvial tin from the stream and river beds, and evidence of these early workings can be seen in most river valleys as heaps of rubble and waste. Streaming was followed by opencast mining, when the ore was refined by the use of water deflected along one leat after another. With the lighter waste thus removed, the remaining 'black tin' was then smelted. Although early smelting was crude, the advent of blowing houses in the 14th century produced a more pure metal. In the 18th century open-cast gave way to shaft mining and pits that once contained water wheels necessary for operating the pumps can still be seen. During the 12th century Dartmoor had been the largest tin-producer in Europe and the industry continued until the 1930s, so a great deal of visible evidence remains - humps and gullies, water channels, heaps of discarded stones, hollowed out granite mortar-stones on which ore was crushed, ruins of blowing houses where tin was smelted, and stone moulds used to form ingots - all tell-tale signs of this once thriving industry.

After smelting, the ingots had to be taken for assaying and payment of tax to one of Devon's stannary towns (from the Latin stannum, meaning tin). Indeed, packhorses carrying tin to one of the four towns formed much of the early traffic on Dartmoor. These towns, Ashburton, Tavistock, Plympton and Chagford, were designated in the 14th century for the administration of stannary laws and each provided 24 jurors for the stannary parliament of Devon, held on Crockern Tor - the centre of all four and close to a pack route. Cornwall held its own on Kit Hill. This was a time when tin miners were in a powerful position and outside normal laws.

Rabbit farming provided a ready source of fresh meat for the large number of miners and remains of their warrens can still be found (mounds of earth-covered stones that were easy to burrow into). They had been brought to this country by the Normans in 1066 and had soon become a useful source of food. The Warren House Inn, which is reputed to have had a fire continuously burning in its hearth since 1845, now stands isolated high up on the moor but it was built to service the three mines in the valley below. Today this valley is completely deserted but, during the 19th century, more than 100 men worked there.

The river port of Morwellham, founded more than 1,000 years ago by the Benedictine monks of Tavistock Abbey, was one of the main ports used for exporting tin from Dartmoor. It later grew to become the greatest copper port in Queen Victoria's empire. Today this charming village, tucked away in the wooded Tamar Valley, is an open-air museum where period costume of the 1860s is the dress of the day. Around the quays are demonstrations and activities ranging from a cooperage to a smithy, and a carpenter's workshop to an assay laboratory. There is even a tram ride into an ancient copper mine that was last worked in 1869 - it is a real spy-hole to days gone by.

The tin industry was responsible for changing the face of Dartmoor, as well as the silting up of the River Plym, the subsequent death of Plympton and the resulting growth of Plymouth.

Morwellham Quay